CATARACTS

NIYOMI H. SHAH

Copyright 2021
Niyomi Shah
All rights reserved
First edition
Design, Editing, and Illustration by Cardy Press

Dedicated to my family for pushing me to new heights I could have never reached without their constant support.

My mom, Shruti: for being a strong talented support who serves as my role model every step of the way

My dad, Himanshu: for being a caring and hard-working individual who encourages me to chase my dreams

My brother, Bhavin: for being a ray of sunshine who motivates me to live life to the fullest

My grandparents, Pravin and Bindu + Kumar and Ila: for being my mentors and backbone throughout my life and inspiring me to publish this book

Foreword

"Eye Wonder" came about because of my great grandmother. When I was young, I used to sit by my grandfather's knee and he would tell me beautiful stories of his childhood with his mother in India. She was beautiful, vibrant, and full of life. She was the mother of 8 children, of which my grandpa was the youngest. Tragedy struck when her eyes became cloudy over time and her sight was taken from her. My grandfather described the fear he felt when he lost his mother. He was in a void… full of darkness because he knew that his mother would never be able to see him again. He had lost himself and he had lost her. As he would tell me these stories, I would wonder what I would do if this happened to my mother. What if she were to lose her sight? How would my life have been? It made me wonder about possible preventative measures even as a child. In middle school I wanted to study science and anatomy, especially the eye. As I came into high school, I devoured every book about the eye to educate myself and lessen my fear. Eventually I was able to shadow multiple ophthalmologists as they cared for patients who suffered from the same malady as my grandmother: cataract. What I learned amazed me. So many of the patients I spoke with as they waited in the lobby for their appointments had the same fears that I had. They wondered if they were going to lose their sight, wondered what could be done to prevent damage, wondered if they were ever going to see the beauty of the world again. I then had the good fortune to watch as the doctors and nurses gave such great care and performed cataract surgery on many of the patients. Pulling a curtain aside to show what happens during that stressful time is part of the mission of this little book. Hoping to put patients at ease, I strived to find answers to their questions. What if I gave them an overview of what cataract surgery would be like? What if I described the process and importance of cataract surgery? What if I looked at what life would be like post-surgery? I wanted to answer all these questions through this book. Simply, to bring a small tool of awareness to take away a little bit of the worry and fear while shedding some light where there is darkness about this subject. Hopefully, in this process, I provide some healing to the worry of cataract that fills the minds of the patients and their loved ones.

Mary was a mother of two and a grandmother to eight. She loved the outdoors, and she would find a way to spare any second of her day taking in the sunlight. She also enjoyed cooking for her grandchildren and spending time with them.

One day as Mary sat down in her white chair, she nervously began wondering what ailed her. The trouble started when she experienced disturbance in her vision. The words in her cooking book started to feel blurred and lights were lined with halos. It all was so foreign to her, and she wondered where she could find some answers. Mary decided to take a trip down to the eye clinic.

After checking-in, Mary sat in a chair lined against the window, twirling a handkerchief in her hand. Suddenly, she was interrupted by a smiling receptionist who offered to talk to her a little about her visit at the office today.

"Hi Mary! My name is Christy. It appears that you may be a little nervous today, but I promise Dr. Patel will take good care of you. I've followed the journey of many other patients and can assure you that at the end of the procedure, the patients are beyond satisfied and pleased with their outcome."

"Thank you, Christy. I look forward to speaking to him."

Just a few seconds later, she heard a voice call her name, and it was time to head back to the exam room.

"Welcome, Mary! My name is Doctor Patel."
"Hi Dr. Patel! I'd like to learn more about cataracts and their causes."
"Great. I can surely help with that. Have a seat. Let me tell you a little bit about it. Here's a chart explaining the three types of cataracts. The progression rate varies based on the type of cataract."

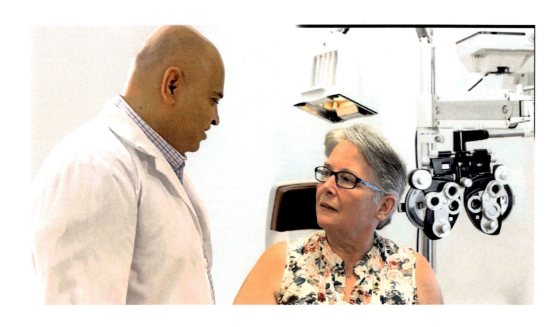

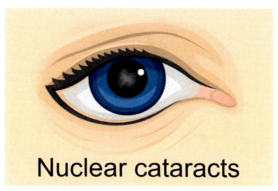

Nuclear cataracts

Nuclear Sclerotic: These types of cataracts form deep in the nucleus of the eye.

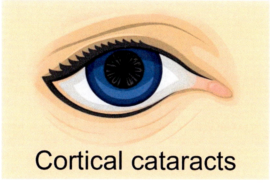

Cortical cataracts

Cortical Cataract: These types of cataracts have white opaque "spokes" that work toward the center, affecting peripheral vision.

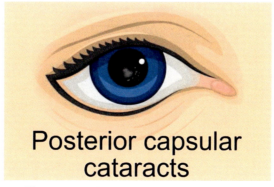

Posterior capsular cataracts

Posterior Capsular: These cataracts are prevalent in patients with diabetes and those who use high doses of steroids.

"Cataracts tend to occur in four different stages, and the progressions vary with each individual. Cataracts are also dependent on factors such as exposure to UV rays, use of medications, and age. This chart explains the various stages of a cataract and how it may progress."

Progression of Cataracts

Stage 1: Normal (The Early Stage)
The early stage consists of the lens remaining clear but the ability to focus and refocus at a distance is lost.
Symptoms - during this stage of cataract you may experience some early signs of cataract such as:

Increasing eye strain
Mild blurring or clouding
Increasing light sensitivity
Early appearance of glare

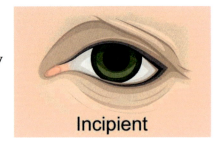
Incipient

Stage 2: Immature Stage

The cataract becomes more prevalent as the opacity of the lens destructs the vision. Light shined from the side can cause the pupil to cast a shadow on the lens.

Symptoms -
Double vision
Dimmed vision
Blurred vision

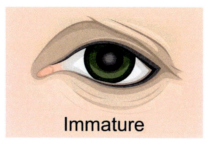

Stage 3: Mature Stage

The lens starts to turn into a complete white or deep amber color and the iris no longer casts a shadow. It is advised that you visit the eye clinic.

Symptoms - similar to those seen in the immature stage, but more severe, quality of life can be affected

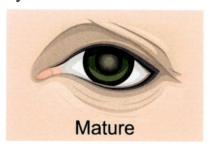

Stage 4: Hypermature Stage

The lens has shrunken quite a bit with white spots apparent. A visit to the eye clinic would be highly recommended.

Symptoms -
Significant blur
Loss of vision

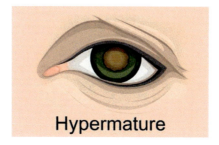

"So how do we remove cataracts?"

"Great question Mary. During the surgery, they make a small minimally invasive incision into the cornea, the clear outer layer of the eye, to break up the cataract. Once the cataract is removed, we place a clear implant that requires no additional care and becomes a part of your eye. This allows focusing of light and images onto the retina, thus improving your vision. More than 28 million people develop cataracts in one or both eyes and more than 4 million get their surgery done through a process called phacoemulsification. It has a wonderful success rate of 99%, and it is simple and very effective."

After hearing this, Mary looked at Dr. Patel and felt relief. Her questions were answered and her fears were dissipated.

"Now Mary, let me examine your eyes so I can let you know what the next steps would be."

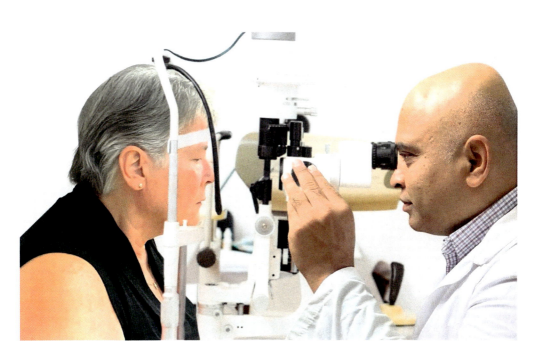

"You do have cataracts, which we can definitely take care of. If you are ready to move on to have your sight improved we can schedule an appointment for the procedure."

"Yes, I would love to get this started. Now that my questions are answered, it feels like my recovery won't be too difficult and everything will be alright."

"Perfect! Look over this for the pre-procedure regimen and don't hesitate to contact me at any time!" he exclaimed as he walked Mary out.

As soon as Mary sat in the car, she felt like she could exhale. For the first time, she was filled with hope and relief.

The morning of the procedure, Mary's husband accompanied her to the clinic. The doctor greeted her with his reassuring manner, "Mary, you'll soon wish that you would have taken care of this years ago. Ready to go? Let's get started."

Mary was taken to get her vitals checked before the procedure.

"Everything looks normal. We are going to dilate your right eye, the one that will be operated on today, and will momentarily give you anesthesia. In the meantime, why don't you take a seat on the surgical chair and relax."

"Sure thing, Dr. Patel!"

A nurse anesthetist named Graciela walked into the room.

"Hi Mary! I will be giving you anesthesia today. This anesthesia is not strong and will keep you mildly asleep."

After the nurse had given Mary the anesthesia, she rolled her into the procedure room. There Mary was greeted with smiling faces and health professionals full of excitement, ready to get the surgery underway.

"Hi Mary! I'm Ria, the scribe, and this is Emily, the technician. We will also be in the room while Dr. Patel is doing the surgery. It looks like we are almost ready to go. Just a few ground rules. Remember, if you have to sneeze or cough, give us a little signal and let us know!"

"Sounds good!"

Emily dimmed the lights in the room and soft, gentle instrumental music filled the quiet, peaceful room as Dr. Patel and the nurse were working on the cataract eye. Mary felt as if she was looking through a kaleidoscope. Light was flashing here and there and she was at ease: relaxed and calm.

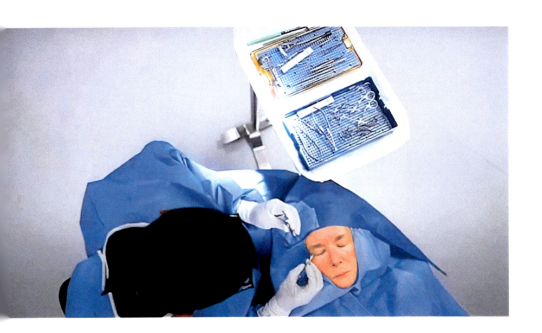

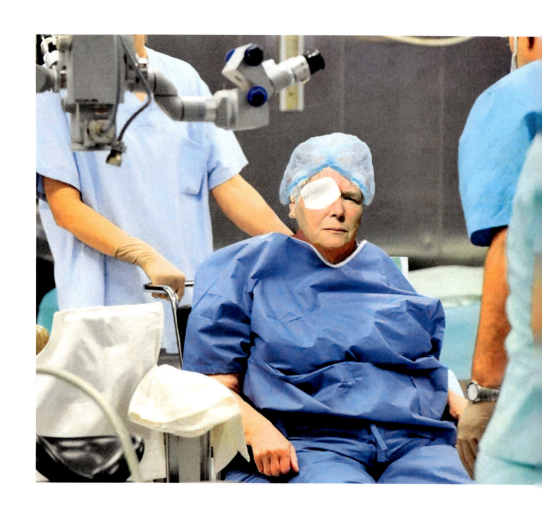

In no time at all, the dark room lit back up. She felt a little tap on her shoulder.

"Mary, we are done. I'm just putting some antiseptic liquid on your eye and covering your eye with a therapeutic bandage. Emily will roll you out and give you some last minute instructions. Have a great day!"

Emily checked Mary's vitals one more time and took off her therapeutic bandage.

"Here are your sunglasses. Everything looks great and you are all set to go. Wear these on your way out."

"Also, remember to follow the post-op directions in the brochures, and we will see you soon."

One week later, Mary returned to the clinic once more for her follow up visit. She couldn't wait to see the doctor. She wanted to let him know how much brighter and clearer things were now.

"Hi Mary! How are you feeling?" asked Dr. Patel as he checked Mary's eye.

"I feel great! I can see 20/20 after such a long time and can finally get back to cooking! I'm so happy I had this taken care of. I just wish I could let everyone know how simple and painless it is to have this done. I do wish I had come sooner."

"I am happy to hear this. Your eyes are healing well. Yes, there are many people every year that avoid cataract surgery for various reasons but at the end of the day, it is worth it for the improved vision."

Mary was beyond satisfied and could not thank Dr. Patel enough.

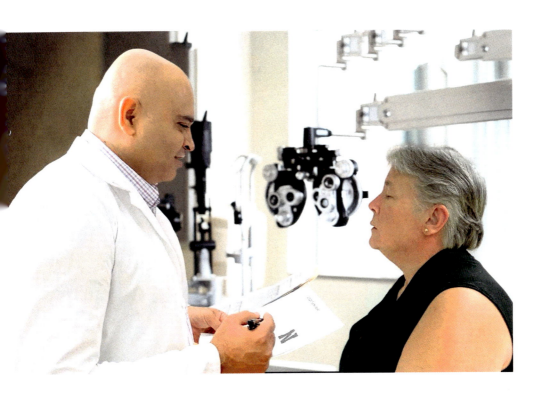

"Well, thank you Mary for allowing me to make a difference and feel free to reach out if you have any trouble with your eye."

"Of course. Thank you."

The doctor smiled with joy as he realized that his lifelong goal of healing was happening, one patient at a time, and today that patient was named Mary.

Acknowledgments

The journey of authoring this book has been one of the most rewarding experiences of my life. It would have not been possible without the support and guidance of so many. I would like to sincerely thank each of the following individuals and organizations for helping my dream become a reality.

Virginia Browning - for being a mentor and a helping hand throughout this journey.

Milan Eye Team & Center - for allowing me to grow my curiosity and love for ophthalmology.

Rotary Club of Johns Creek - for giving me the opportunity to serve the community and connecting me to wonderful people.

Navin Patel, Amit Patel, Chris Allemand, Debra Downen, Felicia Lybrand, and Mansi Bhimani - who have been a part of my getting here and making these beautiful images come to life.

About the Author

Niyomi Shah is a student who has been fascinated by the eye since a very young age due to ocular conditions she endured. She wrote this book to decrease fear for patients diagnosed with cataract and increase their knowledge of this condition. In her freetime, you can catch Niyomi dancing to the tunes of any song, adventuring through nature rain or shine, and serving her community through a club that she has founded.

Check out her website to learn more!
eyewonderbook.com

Made in the USA
Columbia, SC
25 March 2022